HOW TO LEAVE BITCOIN TO YOUR HEIRS

A SIMPLE INHERITANCE PLAN FOR YOUR SELF-CUSTODY BITCOIN

ANTHONY S. PARK

ISBN: 9798868037573

www.anthonyspark.com

Cover design by JD Smith Design

For all the disruptors, rebels, and misfits who are the bitcoin community

THANK YOU FOR YOUR FEEDBACK

Thank you for your feedback

Hearing directly from you, the reader, is the best way for me to make these books as useful as possible.

Please share how this book has helped you, or any suggestions for how I can make it better. You can email me at btcexecutor@anthonyspark.com or call me at 212-401-2990.

Thanks in advance for your feedback.

Best,

Anthony S. Park

CONTENTS

INTRODUCTION

Family, death, and money. When someone dies, the probate process throws all these at you, and it is overwhelming. Now add a wonderful, new, and complicated asset such as bitcoin. As you can probably imagine, inheriting your bitcoin could be a challenge for your heirs—but it doesn't have to be.

WHO THIS BOOK IS FOR

This book is for you if you're a **non-beginner, self-custody bitcoiner thinking about how your heirs will inherit your stack**. So I won't cover the basics of "What is bitcoin?" or "What is self-custody?"

Ideally, you either already hold your bitcoin in self-custody, or you are doing your research and about to make the leap. You either have a singlesig hardware wallet, or you know what it is and plan to get yours soon.

Even if you're more technically advanced and believe you have a sound plan, you'll still benefit from this book. You'll learn about the probate process and how realistically your plan may (or may not) perform upon your death.

How much bitcoin must you own before you need a plan? The basic bitcoin estate plan proposed within this book is simple, easy, and inexpensive. So long as your holdings are large enough to justify purchasing a hardware wallet, this plan may make sense for you.

WHAT YOU'LL GET FROM THIS BOOK

A no-excuses, easy-to-make, frictionless bitcoin estate plan that will actually work when you die. Your plan has just three parts:

1. Name a professional executor.
2. Make a do-it-yourself will.
3. Set up a "poor man's" multisig.

WHEN TO MAKE YOUR PLAN

Now. Immediately. Even if it's just a placeholder until you make a "better" plan later. Because self-custody bitcoin doesn't have any default safety nets. So you must have some plan, *any* plan, that will allow you to avoid catastrophic loss, right now.

WHERE DO YOU LIVE?

This plan is directed to U.S. bitcoiners, even if you have heirs overseas. However, the information on custody transfer and other concepts can be useful to any bitcoiners worldwide.

WHY A BITCOIN INHERITANCE PLAN IS SO IMPORTANT

Unlike legacy assets, there is no default inheritance plan, no safety net, no fail-safe for your bitcoin upon your death. If you don't have a plan, your hard-saved bitcoin may be lost forever, a donation to all other HODLers. So *you* must create your own backup plan. You cannot rely on anyone else.

With legacy assets, I'm not one of those Chicken Little lawyers who dramatically warns that you must have an estate plan. Why not? As I'll describe later, legacy financial assets have plenty of default fail-safes. So in the worst case, even if you have no plan at all, your heirs will eventually inherit and receive your assets, albeit with more headaches and legal costs. Not so with self-custody bitcoin.

Don't worry, that's why you're reading this book: to make sure everyone successfully gets their rightful inheritance.

ABOUT ME AND MY PERSPECTIVE

You probably want to know: "Who is this author? And why should I listen to what he has to say?" Understandable.

I'm *not* a technical bitcoin expert. Rather, I'm more of an interested enthusiast.

But I do have a lot of experience with probate and estates. As a New York professional executor and probate lawyer for over 20 years, I've worked hundreds of probate estates. I've also written books on probate (*How Probate Works*) and executors (*How to Hire a Professional Executor*).

Most folks have never experienced probate firsthand, or at most, one or two cases (such as a parent, an uncle, etc.). Think of me as the power user who has done this many, many times and has seen what *actually* happens upon death, at statistically significant volume.

How did I get involved with bitcoin inheritance and executorship? Like you, I'm intrigued by bitcoin. As I learned about self-custody, it was immediately clear to me (because of my experience with hundreds of probates) that bitcoin probate and inheritance have *huge* potential problems! So I wanted to help.

This is my little contribution back to the bitcoin community. I can't code or develop, but this is what I know, and hopefully, it will help.

THE GOAL OF THIS BOOK

I want to give you a basic bitcoin estate plan that is easy to understand and easy to set up, so you're not walking around without a safety net—and so your heirs will realistically understand how to successfully receive their inheritance.

This guide is not a replacement for legal counsel, and I recommend that you work with an experienced attorney to get personalized advice.

So if I recommend you seek counsel anyway, why bother reading this guide at all?

1. You'll have a real-world understanding of how probate works in general, and why transferring bitcoin self-custody upon death can be so difficult.
2. You may realize that setting up a basic, baselayer bitcoin estate plan that will actually work isn't as complicated as you feared.
3. When you start to work with your attorney, you'll have a basic level of understanding and will have thought through some of the issues ahead of time.

BRIEF OUTLINE

In Chapter 1, we'll briefly go over the basics about estates, probate, and executors.

In Chapters 2 through 4, I'll describe why you must have a plan, and what characteristics will make sure that your plan exists and will work as intended.

In Chapters 5 through 7, I'll explain the steps of your basic bitcoin estate plan and the rationale for each step.

Lastly, in Chapter 8, I'll describe why some of the other popular inheritance ideas are not suitable for your baselayer plan.

Let's get started.

CHAPTER 1

WHAT YOU NEED TO KNOW ABOUT ESTATES, EXECUTORS, AND PROBATE

WHAT IS AN ESTATE?

AN ESTATE IS a person's assets, debts, and tax obligations upon death. Think bank accounts, real estate, mortgage, car, and yes, bitcoin. Then subtract debts such as mortgages, credit card debt, and medical bills. Finally, file and pay any final taxes. The remainder is your net estate, or what your heirs will get.

WHAT IS PROBATE?

After you die, probate is the process through which your jumble of assets, debts, and taxes will be organized into the final net estate to be paid to your heirs. The entire process usually takes at least a year, often much longer.

WHAT IS AN EXECUTOR?

Your executor will be the court-appointed person with the legal authority to conduct the probate process for your estate. The financial institutions that handle your assets, debts, and taxes will only communicate and share information with your executor, not just anyone.

Your executor must submit his certificate of court appointment (or letters testamentary) and your death certificate to banks, brokerages, and the IRS before they'll begin working with him.

WHY IS PROBATE SO HARD?

First, probate is very time-consuming. The average takes 570 hours. Put another way, that's like 71 full work days or 14 full work weeks or three and a half months of work. The average probate also spans at least 16 months. This is a long grind for both your executor and your heirs.

Second, the probate process includes constant legal, tax, and financial decisions that impact your heirs. Your executor is personally liable for all of her decisions, so smart executors are very deliberate when deciding who to hire, when to sell, and what to pay.

Lastly, we have the human element and heir drama. Probate involves relationships among your loved ones, friends, heirs, and executor, mixed with inheritance money at stake. It's very common for old personal biases, grudges, and resentments to surface and add even more complications to the process.

This is just a light summary. For deeper explanations, pick up my other guides *How Probate Works* and *How to Hire an Executor*. Otherwise, let's move on to bitcoin inheritance.

CHAPTER 2

WHY YOU MUST HAVE A BASELAYER PLAN

UNLIKE LEGACY ASSETS, self-custody bitcoin has <u>no safety nets</u>, no default built-in inheritance plan. This means if you have no plan, the downside risk is that your heirs may never receive their inheritance, and your hard-saved bitcoin may be irrevocably lost! So you must create your own basic plan.

With such a catastrophic downside risk in the absence of any plan, it makes sense to have a plan that will actually work upon your death, *even if you hate some of the trade-offs*.

Why do we call it a "baselayer plan?" Because thinking of it as just a baselayer, and not necessarily your ultimate inheritance plan, might mentally help many of you accept an imperfect plan that at least puts *something* in place.

SELF-CUSTODY BITCOIN HAS NO SAFETY NETS

Self-custody bitcoin has no safety nets. What do I mean by safety nets? And how are they missing from self-custody bitcoin?

Let's compare the safety nets for legacy assets, such as bank accounts, stock, and real estate. First, legacy financial accounts will help you recover your password or username if you forget them. Second, upon your death, financial institutions with custody of your assets will transfer them to your heirs (upon receipt of documents such as your death certificate and letters testamentary). And lastly, in the very worst case, if you or your heirs completely forget about an asset, there's a process called unclaimed funds. If your assets appear to be "abandoned," they get transferred to your state's unclaimed department.

Thanks to all the safety nets, even if you fail to properly plan for the transfer of your legacy assets, your heirs should still eventually inherit. Yes, collecting your assets will be time-consuming (e.g., dealing with frustrating bureaucrats, etc.) and may take months, even years before your heirs receive their rightful inheritance. There may also be costs, such as higher attorney fees, or other court procedures. But despite these downsides, your heirs will ultimately recover and receive their inheritance.

As you know, this may not be the case with self-custody bitcoin. If you or your heirs lose access to your private keys, then your bitcoin is permanently lost and unrecoverable.

IT'S OK TO HATE THE TRADE-OFFS

Bitcoiners are typically uncompromising on trustlessness, security, and privacy. I get it, and I sympathize. Unfortunately, it's currently unlikely that you can devise an estate plan that completely avoids all of those things *and* maximizes the odds that your heirs will *actually* receive your bitcoin when you die.

In Chapter 8, I'll review several talked-about inheritance solutions and discuss why each is not sufficiently likely to successfully deliver your bitcoin to your heirs.

I understand that losing some trustlessness, security, or privacy all feels terrible. But none of those is as terrible as your heirs losing access to your hard-staked bitcoin, forever!

Don't let the perfect be the enemy of the good. Accept that (for now) you need a plan that will have trade-offs. And don't stress about it too much, because the bitcoin community will in all likelihood develop even better solutions between now and when you die.

THINK OF THIS PLAN AS JUST A BASELAYER

You may find it helpful to mentally think of this bitcoin estate plan as just a baselayer, rather than something set in stone.

Why? Because if you think of it with too much finality ("This is how my heirs will inherit when I die, so it'd better be perfect!"), making the decision will feel too big, triggering analysis paralysis.

So don't think of your plan as a zero-sum decision. Rather, think of it as your baselayer of fail-safes. You're comfortable it will work, even if you don't like some of the trade-offs. But no worries, because now that you have at least *something* in place, you can focus on those tough decisions to make your "perfect" plan, without worrying you'll get hit by a bus in the meantime.

Ok, now that we agree you must have a baselayer plan, how do we make sure you actually do it?

CHAPTER 3

HOW DO YOU SIMPLIFY YOUR ESTATE PLAN, SO IT WILL ACTUALLY EXIST?

THE BEST BITCOIN inheritance plan is the one that actually exists! I've spoken to too many folks who have ideas for their perfect plan, but when I ask if they've implemented it, it's "still in progress."

Even with legacy assets, most people don't have any plan at all. Everyone seems to know they "should" have a plan, so why don't they? The main reasons range from procrastination (don't judge, we're all guilty) to being intimidated by the tough decisions. And all these reasons are magnified when you add bitcoin to your asset picture. Because with bitcoin, you need not only a legal plan, but a custody plan as well.

WHY SO MANY PEOPLE DON'T HAVE AN ESTATE PLAN

Surveys show nearly everyone acknowledges that an estate plan is important, and you should have one. Yet two thirds of those surveyed don't have any will or estate plan. Why not?

Procrastination

Almost half admit that it's just plain old procrastination. Refreshingly honest. If you're guilty of procrastination on your bitcoin estate plan, just remember that the downside is *way* worse than failing to have a legacy estate plan. So don't procrastinate too long!

Not sure where to begin

25% surveyed are simply not sure where to start. Is the first step organizing your assets? Speaking with friends and family? Choosing estate planning software? Or hiring a lawyer first? All the more confusing when you add in self-custody bitcoin.

Worried about cost

About 15% believe creating an estate plan is too expensive. They're not wrong. The average lawyer fee for creating your estate plan ranges from $1,500 to $3,000. Fees could easily be more expensive in large cities such as New York or San Francisco. Very understandable that folks aren't eager to pay that! And you may suspect even higher fees for something newer and more complicated such as a bitcoin estate plan. Don't worry, the baselayer plan I recommend is *free*! Or nearly so.

Too many decisions

But surely procrastination, confusion, and cost alone aren't enough to stop folks from attending to such an important part of their personal finance and protecting the inheritance of their heirs, children, and loved ones. What's the other major hurdle? Too many tough decisions.

Doing something new and unfamiliar, such as making your estate plan, is a chain of many decisions, such as: Do I hire a lawyer or try to do it myself? How do I find a good lawyer? Which do-it-yourself software should I use? Whom do I choose as my heirs? Who will be my executor?

Don't worry, I recommend a basic bitcoin estate plan that simplifies and removes most of these decisions.

HOW WILL YOUR BITCOIN TRANSFER WHEN YOU DIE?

On top of all the above reasons for not having a plan, imagine you now also need a second, technical plan as well! That's essentially the case with self-custody bitcoin, because on top of your legal documents, you must make arrangements to safely transfer custody of your bitcoin to your executor or heirs upon your death.

Why is transferring bitcoin custody upon death so tough? Remember, there are no safety nets. And the downside risk is complete catastrophic loss of your hoard. No pressure, right? Also, there are no "default" best practices the community seems to agree on. There's no consensus to "get off exchanges" or "use a hardware wallet," etc. that you can rely on.

This baselayer is my humble entry as a default plan that the community can come to consensus around.

I've removed almost all barriers so your plan will actually exist. Now we must make it as flexible as possible, so it will actually work upon your death.

CHAPTER 4

WHY IS FLEXIBILITY IN ESTATE PLANNING SO IMPORTANT?

YOU UNDERSTAND YOU NEED *A* PLAN, and you've overcome all the friction to actually set it up. But will it actually work upon your death? Will it actually succeed and deliver your bitcoin to your heirs? The best way to make sure is to keep your plan flexible and future-proof.

I recommend keeping your legacy estate plan as flexible as possible. Even more so for your bitcoin inheritance plan.

Why flexible? Because it's very hard to predict what circumstances will be when you die. So you want a plan that isn't rigid and can adapt to how the world is when you die, not how you imagined it would be five, ten, or twenty years earlier.

This future-proofing is even more important with bitcoin because it's such a fast-changing technology.

Lastly, with legacy and bitcoin plans alike, there's a strong temptation to try and automate as much as possible. I'll explain why automation is a poor fit for estate planning in general, and bitcoin inheritance in particular.

PREDICTION IS VERY DIFFICULT, ESPECIALLY ABOUT THE FUTURE

Folks tend to make their estate plans in a time vacuum. Meaning, they assume circumstances now will be substantially the same when they die. But more often than not, circumstances are not only mismatched, but wildly different.

What do I mean by circumstances won't match? For example, your net worth may have dramatically increased (or decreased). Let's say you plan to leave your nephew $25,000, which represents 10% of your net worth today. If your net worth fluctuates, that $25,000 could end up being a very different percentage of your total estate in the future.

Or, your relationships with your heirs may have changed quite a bit between when you made your plan and when you die. Maybe you drifted apart, your values have changed and no longer match, trust has been broken, or you've discovered that an heir is now financially unfit.

And of course, the people named in your plan may have died, divorced, or moved away.

You may be thinking: *I'm not worried about those things because I would update my inheritance plan if any of them happened.* Unlikely. Of those surveyed who even have a plan, 70% say their existing plan is not up to date.

Lastly, if you haven't been through several probates, you may not realize the general chaos of an estate. It's very hard, even for experienced professionals, to predict who will fight, who will cause drama, and what debts or taxes will shake up the estate.

HOW QUICKLY WILL NEW TECHNOLOGIES DEVELOP?

On top of these potential changes in our life circumstances, we have to consider that bitcoin is still relatively new and evolving. The underlying core principles may seem etched in stone, but the reality is that the community, environment, and how users adopt and interact with bitcoin is still very much a work in progress.

Think back just a few years, and you may recall things such as paper wallets and pre-BIP39 seed phrases. You can imagine how an outdated inheritance plan based on the technology from those earlier bitcoin periods would be problematic.

Who knows what the future holds?

WHAT IS THE PROBLEM WITH BENEFICIARY DESIGNATIONS?

It's tempting to want to automate as much as possible in your life, because who has the time or mental energy to remember, let alone do, everything these days? But too often, inheritance automations, such as beneficiary designations, simply don't work as intended.

If you've tried to automate things in your business or personal life, you probably already know that automation is best suited for predictable, repeating tasks rather than things that require real-time decision-making. In your personal life, you may automate regular tasks (e.g., monthly bill pay, direct deposit payroll, automatic savings) versus one-off tasks such as scheduling doctor appointments, planning a vacation, and even grocery shopping. Similarly, in business, automation is fine for repeating tasks such as social media posts and vendor payment, but not so much for customer service.

An automation can't make decisions, adjust to current circumstances, or keep itself up to date. It simply executes your instruction, even if it no longer makes sense. For example, if you've filed for divorce but it's not yet finalized, and your soon-to-be-ex-spouse is still named beneficiary on your 401k, she still inherits your retirement account!

Why are beneficiary designations particularly prone to being out of date? Because there are no conspicuous reminders of whom you've named as beneficiaries. Or that you ever named a beneficiary at all. It's not on your account statements, and you often must click through several times to find out on your online account.

For all these reasons, I generally don't recommend relying on beneficiary designations in any estate plan, and definitely not with your bitcoin estate plan.

So what *do* I recommend instead? Here we go.

CHAPTER 5

STEP ONE: NAME A PROFESSIONAL EXECUTOR

FIRST, you'll skip the tough decision-making and simply name a professional executor to be in charge upon your death.

WHY IS AN EXECUTOR BETTER THAN AUTOMATING?

When you die, a live human decision-maker can adjust and adapt to the situation as needed, versus automations.

Your executor will decide things like how hard to fight a will contest, which estate assets to liquidate or keep to pay debts and expenses, and any other adjustments to make sure your estate matches your actual intentions as closely as possible.

Your executor will also do all the other necessary probate jobs that aren't just about who inherits. Jobs like cleaning out and staging real estate; closing and collecting all accounts; and paying expenses, creditors, and taxes. And yes, gaining and securely maintaining custody of your bitcoin for your heirs during the long probate process.

HIRE A PROFESSIONAL TO SKIP TOUGH DECISIONS

Choosing your executor is one of the tough decisions that stalls your estate plan. Why? Because your executor must have the following traits:

1. **Understands probate law and won't get bullied on decisions.** Your bitcoin executor must know her rights to stick as closely as possible to your wishes. Such as not to sell your bitcoin for fiat, not to move it onto a centralized exchange, and to keep it self-custody.

2. **Understands tax law and tax audits.** The IRS doesn't mess around when someone dies. They know this is their "last bite at the apple," and they examine final taxes very closely, even aggressively. So a good executor knows how to handle capital gains from trading, stepped-up basis, and inheritance and estate income taxes.

3. **Has enough free time and energy.** Being an executor is a long and time-consuming job. This isn't something to just put on your pal from weekly bitcoin meetups; it's a big ask. Not only does it take a lot of time, it's also frustrating because all the steps and bureaucracies are very archaic and chaotic (for more details, read my other books *How Probate Works* and *How to Hire a Professional Executor*.)

4. **Is not also an heir, ideally with no personal relationship with the heirs.** This

is to avoid pre-existing personal biases and possible drama during probate. It's also important to split and separate the "keys" of your bitcoin custody among people who don't know each other (see Chapter 7 for more detail).

5. **Understands bitcoin custody.** Because this person will be in charge of gaining custody upon your death. And also maintaining secure custody throughout the months or years of the long probate process.

As you can see, it's not like choosing your best man or maid of honor, or just whoever's closest to you. Most people will struggle to think of someone who checks all these boxes, so just name a professional executor like me as your bitcoin executor as a placeholder for now. This eliminates the friction of struggling to think of someone.

And I really mean just a placeholder. You'll probably live a long time. Hopefully long enough for friends or family to satisfactorily learn about bitcoin on their own. Or better yet, long enough for better solutions to develop that don't rely on any executor or any third party.

BUT HOW MUCH DOES A PROFESSIONAL EXECUTOR COST?

Nominating a professional executor doesn't cost anything now. And upon your death, executor fees are the same whether your executor is a professional or an amateur nephew who has no idea how probate works.

An executor doesn't earn a fee simply by being named in your will or trust. There is *no fee* owed at the moment you name your executor, only upon your death.

And even if you die with a professional executor in place, in most states the statutory fee for an executor is exactly the same whether it's an experienced professional or your amateur buddy. So may as well get the pro!

HOW TO LEVEL UP

Once your baselayer plan, and therefore your safety net, is in place, you can start thinking about leveling up.

Over time, hopefully a friend, family member, or lawyer will emerge who checks all the boxes as your executor. Even when that happens, you can still keep me (or someone like me) as your successor executor, a redundant backup.

Once you've decided who'll be in charge when you die, the next step is to legally nominate your executor by making your will.

CHAPTER 6

STEP TWO: MAKE A DO-IT-YOURSELF WILL

NEXT, you need a legal document to formally nominate your executor. This is the legal part of your plan. You'll use free websites to create your own will, but hire a local attorney to make sure you sign, witness, and notarize it properly. And you'll do a few things to make sure your will doesn't reduce your privacy or your heirs'.

WHY YOU NEED A DIY WILL

Your basic bitcoin will is do-it-yourself to make it as easy as possible—so you'll actually do it. The two biggest sources of friction preventing most people from making their will are: the many tough decisions, and cost. So I've removed nearly all decisions for you *and* minimized costs.

No need to research or ask your friends for referrals, just go to https://www.freewill.com and use their professionally made web-based software to create your own simple will. I have no affiliation with the site. I believe it is maintained by large charities (which explains why there are so many prompts asking if you'd like to leave something to charity). I've tested the site for simple bitcoin wills, and it works well.

(I also tested https://www.doyourownwill.com as an alternative. It's also fine, but I noticed a few typos in the will. Not critical errors, but not quite as polished.)

Ignore the self-signing instructions, and don't try to sign your will by yourself. Too many clients make errors with signing, witnessing, or notarizing that render the will invalid. Instead, hire a local attorney to supervise your will signing.

HIRE AN ATTORNEY, BUT JUST TO SUPERVISE SIGNING

Most folks don't realize there are particular requirements to properly sign, witness, and notarize your will. And if you screw those up, your will is invalid.

The attorney will also provide professional witnesses, usually their experienced paralegals or other office staff who will make great witnesses if anyone contests your will. They're much better witnesses than the UPS driver or random bank teller you probably would have used if you tried signing on your own.

I've also seen firsthand that probate court clerks give much more respect to attorney-supervised wills. Whereas when I submit to the court a will that was not supervised by a lawyer, the court clerk will roll her eyes and give the will a much tougher examination to get through probate.

So pay a local estate lawyer to supervise. It should cost $100 to $300, still just a fraction of the cost of a full estate plan, and very much worth it.

KEEP YOUR BITCOIN PRIVATE

Lastly, how you write and store your will can help keep your bitcoin more private and safe.

There's no need to explicitly mention the word "bitcoin" anywhere in your will. When describing each heir's inheritance, just use broad percentages (examples: 50% to my son, 50% to my daughter) rather than listing specific assets (my Apple stock to my son, my bitcoin to my daughter).

This also helps protect your heirs when you die. During probate, your will becomes part of the public court record, which anyone can see. So obviously don't write your seed phrase in your will. And even mentioning that your heir is inheriting bitcoin puts a target on her back to hackers, scammers, and other unsavory types.

Once your will is complete and properly signed, where should you keep it? Give the original to your non-heir executor for safekeeping. An experienced professional executor or lawyer will have fire-proof storage for just this reason.

Don't keep the original yourself, because if anything happens to the original, the law assumes you intentionally destroyed and revoked it. If someone else was holding onto it, since they don't have the right to revoke your will, your heirs may still probate a copy of your will, even without the original.

And don't stick it in your safe deposit box. You generally need the will to gain access to a deceased person's safe deposit box, so if the will is inside, it creates a bit of a catch-22.

HOW TO LEVEL UP

Once you've made your DIY, how can you improve on this baselayer plan?

When it's cost-justified, hire a lawyer to prepare your entire plan, not just supervise the signing. Your lawyer-prepared plan may include a trust, not just a will. In many states, a trust can add even better privacy by avoiding the probate court public records altogether.

Now, on to the last step of your basic bitcoin estate plan: how to transfer custody of your bitcoin upon your death.

CHAPTER 7

STEP 3: SET UP A "POOR MAN'S MULTISIG"

FINALLY, the bitcoin custody part of your plan. Now that you've chosen who'll be in charge and have a legally binding document appointing him, it's time to set up how your executor will get custody of your bitcoin when you die.

Use a single-sign wallet with an added passphrase (sometimes called "the 25th word"). This is a good enough balance of convenience for you now, but also a split multifactor for your heirs later. Hence the nickname "poor man's multisig."

CONVENIENT TRANSACTIONS WHILE YOU'RE STILL ALIVE

Any bitcoin estate plan must not unduly hinder your ability to transact conveniently while you're alive.

Many attempted solutions to bitcoin inheritance essentially lock up your funds while you're alive. In Chapter 8, I'll explain how Shamir's Secret Sharing, deadman switches, and timelocks all suffer from this. By contrast, a wallet with a passphrase is very easy for you to continue to use. The added inconvenience (entering your passphrase) is negligible, no more inconvenient than the commonly used 2-factor authentication with your legacy bank or even email accounts.

Passphrases are also well established and supported. This means there's no steep learning curve for you to research how to use it or set it up. It's well supported and understood. Even total beginner bitcoiners can figure out how to add a passphrase with some light online research.

And because it's so well established, your executor will have a much higher chance of successfully reconstituting access to your bitcoin upon your passing without risk of complications. Or worse, failure to recover.

WHY YOU NEED TO "MULTIFACTOR" YOUR SEED

Keeping access to your bitcoin wallet all within a single seed phrase is too insecure. In Chapter 8, I'll discuss how sharing your seed phrase in its entirety with an heir or executor is a poor inheritance plan for just this reason.

If you, or your executor or heirs, err and accidentally reveal or lose the seed, that one mistake is enough to put your entire wallet at risk. By splitting access into multifactor, two mistakes or breaches must occur to expose your wallet. By now we're all familiar with 2-factor authentication (SMS + email, etc.) for our bank accounts. Your poor man's multisig uses the same concept.

WITH WHOM TO SHARE THE PARTS?

Keep it simple and share your seed phrase with your heirs (and successor heirs), and your passphrase with your executor and successors.

I agree, sharing your seed phrase can feel nerve-wracking at first. Just remember, your seed phrase by itself is not enough to access your real bitcoin wallet. So you'll share your seed phrase with multiple heirs to create redundancies, since it's hard to predict which heir may lose their copy by the time you die.

You probably now realize why you chose a non-heir executor. You're sharing your passphrase with your non-heir executor to separate the parts needed to reconstitute access to your wallet. There'd be no split possession if your executors and heirs were the same person.

I even recommend you choose professional executors with no personal relationship with your heirs to avoid even the slightest doubt that they might conspire against you and combine your seed and passphrases while you're still alive. So don't choose your best friend who knows your family well.

Upon your death, your professional bitcoin executor, who is familiar with self-custody, will easily gain access to your wallet by gathering the seed phrase from any one of your heirs and combining it with the passphrase he holds.

HOW TO LEVEL UP

Is your stack growing to a size where you want a more robust plan than this baselayer?

Consider a professionally supported multisig wallet instead. Not a do-it-yourself multsig, which is not yet robust enough to avoid problems upon your death. Instead, take a look at some of the collaborative custody multisig companies.

That's the baselayer plan I recommend based on the hundreds of probates I've seen. You may be wondering: *Why not some of the other solutions discussed on Twitter, Reddit, and other forums?* Next, I'll explain why none of those are suitable as your baselayer safety net.

CHAPTER 8

OTHER SOLUTIONS I CAUTION AGAINST (FOR NOW)

THESE COMMON IDEAS may be worth a try as additional layers on top of your baselayer, but you can't rely on them as the foundation for your bitcoin estate plan.

SHARING YOUR SEED PHRASE

Why not just give a copy of your seed phrase to your spouse, adult child, best friend, or someone else you totally trust? It's much simpler than a passphrase or multisig, right?

Yes, sharing your seed phrase is easy. Just hand them a copy. But, it has some risks.

Relationships change. You may have 100% faith in your spouse or child at this moment, but sadly, that may change. Divorce is common. So is growing estranged from family members or falling out with them over money. Now, imagine that estranged family member has a copy of the keys to all your bitcoin! Or, less dramatic, perhaps you come to realize your loved one is just not great with money or technical tasks (such as reconstituting a wallet from a seed phrase).

Even if your relationships remain great, will your heirs know how to safeguard their copy of **your** seed phrase? It's unlikely they will have the same diligence as a fully orange-pilled bitcoiner. Your spouse may be faithful and trust-worthy enough to not steal your funds, but will she remember not to save her copy of your seed phrase on an internet-connected device? Will she save it into an online password manager? Will she simply lose that laminated seed phrase card?

Once you've shared any secret, you can't take it back. So if any of the above problems arise, then you have no choice but to transfer your entire wallet to a new seed phrase. This could be unwieldy and even expensive, depending on trans-action fees at that time.

Lastly, you may have thought about sharing a cloned hard-ware wallet with your heir, rather than a raw copy of your seed phrase. This would help somewhat mitigate the risk of poor security handling by your heir. And a PIN code on the hardware wallet is sort of like a multifactor key. However, it's unlikely your heirs will keep their wallet firmware up to date. And if any significant time passes, even the best hard-ware wallets become at risk for device failure (just like that expensive external hard drive or USB drive with all the family photos failed when you needed it most!).

LETTERS OF INSTRUCTION DON'T WORK

Maybe you plan on writing a detailed letter of instruction to guide your heirs through self-custody after you die. Over hundreds of probates, I've seen firsthand that letters of instruction usually don't work, even with more familiar legacy assets such as small businesses, art, or collectibles.

Owners leave their heirs what they think are clearly written instructions for taking possession of, protecting, and maximizing the value of assets. But with the emotions and stress that come with a loved one's death, many heirs fumble and eventually rely heavily on third parties to help. Sometimes heirs make crucial errors, even with outside help.

Why don't letters work? Two main reasons: the heirs are unmotivated learners, and many letters devolve into a treasure map.

First, most of us are terrible students when we're not interested in the subject. Even when there are thousands or even millions of inheritance dollars at stake, a disinterested heir's eyes can glaze over when trying to learn how to take over a small business or auction off a valuable piece of art. They'd much rather rely on consultants or vendors than drudge through the learning process themselves.

Remember when you first started learning about bitcoin. It might have felt like drinking from a firehose of new information. Now imagine your heir, who has zero interest in the topic except to get her inheritance, trying to learn all that. All while grieving, stressed, and overwhelmed.

Second, too many letters of instruction are poor treasure maps. "The key to my safe deposit box is in my office desk." "My diamond earrings are hidden in the freezer." "$30,000 cash is under a floorboard 12 feet from my bedroom window." I've read many of these letters after death, and few of them actually work.

Why? Because you won't keep the letter up to date. You'll move or change something during your life, so something won't be where the map says it's supposed to be. Which will make the map useless and a frustrating waste of time for your executor or heirs.

DEADMAN SWITCH, SHAMIR'S SECRET SHARING, AND TIMELOCKS

These three techniques are often mentioned as potentially elegant solutions, but unfortunately we don't yet have options to make any work well for bitcoin inheritance.

A deadman switch is any mechanism or protocol that gets activated in the *absence* of activity. For example, if you fail to reply to a series of emails or texts, the deadman switch will eventually assume you've died and trigger. It's the opposite of a proactive action, such as pulling a trigger, pressing a button, etc.

A **transaction deadman switch** will execute a transaction when triggered, such as sending all the contents of your bitcoin wallet to your heir.

A **secret deadman switch** will deliver a secret when triggered, such as sending your seed phrase to your heirs.

Shamir's Secret Sharing is a method for sharing parts of a secret among a group. Similar to multisig, the secret is not revealed unless a minimum number of group members share their parts.

A **timelock** is similar to a deadman switch, where a transaction or secret is triggered once a set amount of time has passed.

All are theoretically attractive because they don't require a trusted third party. Unfortunately, they're also unlikely to work as intended because of failed automation, asking too much of your heirs, locking up your funds, and other security concerns,

Deadman switches and timelocks are essentially beneficiary designations on your bitcoin wallet, and have the same automation drawbacks as beneficiaries named on legacy accounts, discussed in Chapter 4.

For transaction deadman switches and timelocks, your heir must have and maintain a destination address. This has three problems. First, if the intended recipient ever updates, changes, or loses their wallet, your bitcoin will be sent to an incorrect or inaccessible address and could be unrecoverable. Second, there's also the risk your heir does not fully understand self-custody and may lose access or expose their wallet to bad actors who could sweep the entire contents as soon as your bitcoin is delivered. Lastly, you must ask your heir for their destination address, necessarily informing them that they will one day inherit. You may not want to reveal that information just yet.

A transaction deadman switch, Shamir's Secret, and time-lock all lock your funds into a wallet address, or UTXO. You must apply the deadman switch to each of your wallets, and possibly even more incrementally to all of your addresses or UTXOs. So you'd have to update your deadman switch anytime you change wallets, or worse, every time you change or add a new address or UTXO.

A secret deadman switch requires you to type your seed phrase on an internet-connected device. And you already know that's a terrible security risk, since malware and hackers are constantly scanning for seed phrases on any internet-connected device.

What's more, at the time of this writing, there aren't any user-friendly solutions for any of these strategies. They are all very new, and not yet well supported or developed. For example, standards for how to set up and recover a Shamir's Secret are new and still developing. So if you set up your Shamir's Secret now, you might be doing so in a way that puts your seed at greater risk of exposure, or worse, renders it unrecoverable by you or your heirs.

Hopefully, technology will continue to develop and some of these will become viable baselayer inheritance plan options soon.

CHAPTER 9

NEXT STEPS

THAT'S IT! I hope this guide will help you put into place at least your baselayer bitcoin inheritance plan.

I'd love to hear your thoughts and experiences. Please let me know if you make your basic bitcoin estate plan following this guide, or if something else, why? Email me at btcexecu tor@anthonyspark.com with any questions of feedback.

Thank you for reading.

IF YOU LIKED THIS BOOK ...

Thanks for reading. If you enjoyed this book, I'd appreciate a short review. Please consider leaving your honest review on Amazon or your favorite store.

And join my email list for new book announcements: https://anthonyspark.com/join-books/.

ABOUT THE AUTHOR

Anthony is a New York executor, attorney, and entrepreneur. His cases have been featured in many places, including the *Wall Street Journal*, *New York Times*, CNBC, and *MarketWatch*.

Anthony has presented bitcoin inheritance workshops at Adopting Bitcoin in El Salvador, as well as at meetups all over the US. To learn more, visit http://www.anthonyspark. com/.

ALSO BY ANTHONY S. PARK

How to Buy Your Perfect First Home: What Every First-Time Homebuyer Needs to Know

How Probate Works: A Guide for Executors, Heirs, and Families

How to Hire an Executor: For Your Loved One's Estate or Your Will

How to Get Promoted: Simple Steps to Better Title and Higher Pay

How to Invest for Retirement: A Simple Path to Retiring Rich, Independent, and Free

The Solo Ager Estate Plan: Trust and Estate Essentials for Single, Childless Seniors